MW00977265

Reflections

Poems by
Peggy Trojan

Reflections © 2024 by Peggy Trojan

All rights reserved.

Except for quotations and excerpts appearing in reviews, this work may not be reproduced or transmitted, in whole or in part, by any means whatsoever, without prior written permission from the author.

ISBN: 978-1-886895-61-4

Cover photo: Jesse Gram
Cover design: Charlie Gram

Copies of this chapbook are available on *amazon.com*

CONTENTS

Air Mail

I smile to remember
our eyes meeting
across the room,
your finger casually
brushing your lip,
sending a kiss.

Talking Stick   2021

All Relative

"I wish I was sixty-five again,"
I whined in my seventies.
"I know what you mean,"
Pa agreed,
pushing ninety-nine.
"I wish I was eighty-five again."

Talking Stick   2020
Your Daily Poem   2023

Chores

Mother picked up after my father
for sixty-nine years.
I questioned her diligence once.

"Well, " she smiled, "It's easier
to pick up after a good man
than it is to find a good man
in the first place."

Talking Stick 2024

Coinage, 1940s

We called them lead pennies,
but really they were steel
coated with zinc.
All the copper was needed
for the war.
No count was kept
of the steel coins made,
but only forty copper pennies
remain from 1943.
We didn't care much.
A penny was a penny,
good for a choice
from the candy counter
in Webster's store.

Goose River Anthology   2023

Concert

The pine was teeming
with little birds
chirping and tweeting
in afternoon rehearsal.
The doe rested in the shade,
watching her spotted fawn
dance to the spring music.

Cable Library   2022

Connection

When Charlie was five,
he visited his great-great-grandfather
in the nursing home,
when Pa, at ninety-eight, was fading.

He brought a piece of pine bark,
held it to Pa's nose
to let him remember,
then put it in Pa's big hand.

Wisdom ancient as pines
let him know
the old man just wanted
to go home to the woods.

Ariel Anthology   2019

Crayons

In kindergarten in 1937
I could name all the colors
in my Crayola box.
Black, Brown, Yellow, Red,
Blue, Green, Orange, and Violet.
Colors unchanged since 1903.

My children had choices
from boxes of 24, 48, or 64.
Names like Denim, Robin's Egg,
Antique Brass, Tumbleweed,
Macaroni and Cheese, Outer Space,
or Razzmatazz, the winning entry
by a five-year-old in a naming contest.

Today, a child can choose
colors from a box of 120.
If they could identify 40 of these,
I believe they may qualify
for Mensa!

Goose River Anthology   2023

Dolls, 1940s

I got a new doll every year
for Christmas.
I dressed them, fed them,
put them to bed at night.
One generic baby doll
with a soft muslin body
had a little device inside
that made a short cry
when she was bent forward.
The others did nothing
but look at me and smile.

I referred to them
by their brand names—
my Shirley Temple, my Patsy,
my Horseman with her beautiful
blonde mohair wig,
and my Magic Skin doll.

When I confessed to my daughter
that I hadn't given them
their own names,
she said that wasn't very motherly.

Childhood (Pure Slush) 2021

Ducks, 1944

We named them
Huey, Dewey and Louie,
after Donald's clan.
They waddled over
the yard all summer,
eating bugs and grass.

In late fall, when they
were grown and fat,
someone stole two.
Pa killed Huey,
which was probably
the original war food plan,
and hung him
upside down
in the cold back porch
to age for a couple of days.

When he appeared
at the table
on Gramma's old platter,
all crispy brown,
minus his head and wide feet,
none of us kids
would eat him.

Goose River Anthology 2023

Man of Many Hats

Most of David's hats
symbolized a
major accomplishment.

Marine Officer's dress whites
or blue covers, worn with pride.
Marine Helicopter Squadron patch
on another, celebrating twenty-one
years as a pilot.

PhD, gold-tasseled, displayed
twenty years when faculty
marched during University commencement.

Deer hunting, wool with ear flaps,
first red, then blaze orange.
Forty years hunting with my father.

Sophia University hat
for the year he chaperoned
exchange students
while teaching in Tokyo.

Brimmed straw, backpacking
by himself in Mexico,
after a summer teaching
assignment at Monterey
Institute of Technology.

Multiple disposable white painter's hats
worn throughout five years of
building our own retirement home.

Zenith Aircraft Builder's hat,
reflecting his six-year project
completing an all-aluminum
two-seater by himself.
A Zodiac plane he flew proudly for years.

A Navy Nike ball cap
during memory care with Lewy Body.
At eighty-seven, a life well-lived.

Achievement (Pure Slush)   2023

I Confess

My poems are
wee little gifts for you,
or a slap up the side
of the head.
Depends.

Talking Stick 2022

Marriage Bed

I sleep in half-wasted bed,
you in memory care,
I in my new apartment.

I stay on my own side,
having learned over six decades
what boundaries are.

Wisconsin Poets' Calendar 2023

Mentor

Seventy-seven, I enrolled
in a poetry class for seniors.
Jan Chronister, the instructor, told me
I needed to send in my work.
One assignment, "A day I will remember."
I wrote about the end of World War II,
submitted "August 1945,"
Became a published poet.

For the past thirteen years
Jan has continued to teach me,
as a friend and fellow poet.
We attend conferences together,
often present joint readings.
Edit each other's work,
applaud publications and awards.

When she talks, I hear:
Be honest and brave.
Get to the point.
Cut unnecessary words.
Write what you know and feel.
Don't get cute. Keep it simple.
Send it in.

It's working for me.
I think in poetry.

Wilda Morris' Poetry Challenge April 2023

Milwaukee Rain

Driving at night in a downpour.
reflections of headlights,
taillights, stop lights, city lights
created a white knuckle challenge
in a frenzy of shine.

Wisconsin Poets' Calendar 2025

My Wish

When I was eight
the world was at war.
I felt sorry for the children,
wished I could save them
from the cold, from hunger,
pain and fear.
I wished fervently, prayerfully.

That war ended in 1945.
The world continues to fight.
I have been wishing
for over eighty years.

Wilda Morris' Poetry Challenge January 2023

News from Home

I marvel I can send news from Wisconsin
to a daughter on an island in Florida in seconds.
When Grandpa Victor came to America,
it took three months for a letter to come
from Helsinki by boat, then train,
to Moose Lake, Minnesota,
finally by horse and buggy to Lawler,
to tell him his mother had died.

Talking Stick   2022

Open Door

You and your house gone years.
We can see across the empty yard,
all the way down to the little kid's creek.
The oak Ma planted from an acorn
in her seventies now towers sixty feet.
The old rail fence still stands.
Phlox, iris and daffodils bloom every summer,
inviting us to walk the few steps,
enter your front door without knocking.

PA (Poetry Harbor)   2023

Play House

In the early forties
when I was a girl
we played house for hours.
We used my miniature dishes,
silverware and cooking pots,
made mud cakes
with seed decorations.
Dressed and fed our dolls,
washed their little clothes.
All practiced roles
we would fill as adults.
Boys were not allowed
in our house.

By the time my daughters
played in the basement,
roles had changed.
When the girls invited their brother
to join them, he was willing
for a short time
though I heard him complain once,
"How come I always have to be
the Daddy or the dog?"

Growing Up (Pure Slush) 2022

Poems Crowd My Mind

Some, like young children,
jump up and down shouting,
"Look at me!"

Others, more mature,
whisper around my pillow at night
to remind me they are waiting.

Some, so old
they remember mountains
opened by the light,
and my refusal to be a rock
for a hundred million years.

Thunderbird Review 2021

Postcards

Before cell phones,
travelers sent postcards.
My father always bought cards
on his business trips.
Mother found them in his suitcase
when he returned home.
She saved them in her scrapbook
with cards she got in the mail.
We have a pictorial record
of my father's trips.
We assume he was having
a good time and wished
we were there.

Goose River Anthology   2021

Praise for the Double Bed

The double bed we slept in
for over fifty years
contributed to our marriage
in its quiet reliable way.
One hundred twenty-five years old
when we bought it in the sixties,
already had a history of dependability.

Mahogany with five-foot posters,
it provided a visual picture of boundary,
even in soft moonlight.
Allowed easy cuddle, intimate conversations.
If David went to bed before I did,
he often warmed my side with intention.
If we went to sleep with unresolved anger,
an accidental touch during the night
could easily be accepted as an apology.
I would gently poke him to stop snoring.
Would answer when he talked while dreaming,
or check on his breathing when he was ill.
He often touched my shoulder in the night,
making sure I was still there.

Once, he called out quietly,
from a dark king-sized motel expanse,
"Peggy, where are you?"

Marriage (Pure Slush)   2022

Road Trip

We rose eagerly at five
to get on the road,
joined the obedient traffic
leaving Atlanta.
Six lanes,
metal segmented snakes
as far as you could see.
Everyone getting an early start
to beat the morning rush.

Talking Stick   2023

Semper Fi

In the last months,
hospice sent a music therapist
to sing for you.
Knowing your twenty-one year service,
she sang all four verses
of the Marines' Hymn.
We saw the tears in your eyes,
watched your spirit stand at attention
and salute.

Your Daily Poem   Veteran's Day 2023

Sharing an Order

Waitresses often
think it quaint
that Dave and I share orders,
not understanding
we have done this for thirty years
in an effort to limit
our waistlines.
We remind them to bring
only one roll,
often can't finish our half
of the meal.
Once we ordered one piece of pie
after dinner and the waitress
proudly served it
with two forks,
surrounded by a heart
of whipped cream.

Goose River Anthology   2023

Sherri

If you can find
a parking place and table,
Sherri will greet you
across the noisy crowd.

While you are deciding or eating
will come round to give hugs,
kiss the top of your husband's head.
She calls us all sweetheart
or honey and we eat it up.

In the same place on U.S. Hwy. 2
since the thirties,
Twin Gables has been
through wars and fires and
different owners
but it has never buzzed like now.

Sherri isn't just peddling food,
she's serving home-cooked happy.

Wisconsin Poets' Calendar 2019

Siri and Me

I ask a lot of her.
Set the timer,
word definitions,
home remedies for bee stings,
the age of Robert Redford,
when do the Packers play.
When I thank her,
my daughter laughs and reminds me
that no one is there.
But Siri is so polite.
Once she said,
"I didn't quite get that."
I railed at her, letting
her know I didn't
finish my question.
She replied, "That's not very nice."

Thunderbird Review 2021
Your Daily Poem 2024

Small Talk

The crow and the squirrel
who claim the large tree
outside my balcony
meet each morning
to pontificate.
Sometimes I join them.

This morning,
speaking three different languages,
we agreed the weather
has been lousy lately,
and we sure as heck don't need
any more rain.

Bramble 2020
Your Daily Poem November 13, 2022

Spare Change

We did not get an allowance
in the forties
when a bottle of pop or a candy bar
cost a nickel.
We did chores around the house
like a penny for a swatted fly.
(A job which ended when Pa
discovered that we were killing
flies on the outside of the screen door.)
The ideal place for change was between
the brown mohair couch cushions after Pa's
daily noon nap on a lunch break
as manager of the general store.
Looking back now, I suspect he
was intentionally leaving some extra
change, knowing how delighted we
would be upon discovery.

Goose River Anthology   2023

Story Hour

Growing old is a challenge
for most people.
At ninety-one, mine is
macular degeneration.
I no longer read easily.
Years ago, I gave up reading books.
Audrey, my friend for over fifty years,
offered to read over the phone to me.
We meet on most weeknights.

We take turns choosing the books:
best sellers, Pulitzer Prize winners,
old favorites, whatever suits our fancy.
One, a book Audrey gave me fifty years
ago, the ultimate re-gifting.

Sharing a book with a friend
differs from hearing it on tape.
It allows us to visit, to remember
times in our lives that match the story.
Our reading sessions give us both
a social hour in the best of ways.

Our time together is so much more
than the book, a connection between
two friends who no longer drive.
It is a chance to learn, to laugh,
to be reminded of who we are.

Older (Pure Slush)   2024

Surprise

All my long life,
I have been proud
to be one hundred percent Finnish.
Even bragged about it.

When brother Jerry had our DNA done,
we discovered a scandal in the family.
Imagine my shock—
I am one percent Swedish!
One percent!

I am resigned.
Navajo women wove a mistake
into their blankets,
assuring the gods
they were not perfect.

Ariel Anthology 2020
The Dance 2023

Swimming Hole, 1942

We swam in the Brule
down by the park
as it rippled through town
on the way to Lake Superior.
Spring fed, frigid year-round.

Big boys cannonballed
from the bridge.
We girls, in our
winter white skin,
waded in to our waists,
ducked under and hurried out,
shrieking for our towels.
Nancy, on the bank, yelled,
"Virginia, if you go into that whirlpool
and drown, Mother will never let
you come swimming again."

Ariel Anthology 2021

The Sommelier

The bushes were loaded
with wild elderberries.
I thought it was a good time
to try making wine.

I found a recipe,
assembled utensils,
followed directions.

When aged to "perfection,"
I invited my brother John
to be my sommelier.

He swirled his glass
like a professional,
took a sip.
"Well," he said sympathetically,
"it wasn't a good year
for elderberries."

The Thunderbird Review 2024

The Swing

Pa made me a swing
from a wooden box.
Just big enough
for me and a doll or two.

If I stood and pumped,
I could swing for awhile.
Mostly, I was content
to sit suspended in shade
and my imagination.

Goose River Anthology 2021

The Trestle

When I was nine
the world was at war.
I had nightmares
about that at times
but the scariest act
I could think of
was venturing onto
the railroad trestle
high over the river,
no railings.
The boys dared us
to walk across.
In the middle you could see
the rushing water
through the ties.
It made you dizzy.
If a locomotive had
come shooting from town
we would have had to lie down
between the rails
and let the whole train run
over the top of us,
like in the movies.

Goose River Anthology   2023

West on I-40

On the way to California.
Miles and miles
of sand, rock, sage brush.
Looking out the window,
I saw them.

The man walking.
His gaze on the ground. Wondering
if he made the right decision.

The oxen, loyal, patient.
On the other side,
the boy and sister, missing friends.
Everyone thirsty.

The wagon. Huge. Like a boat
covered with grayed white sail.
Essentials. Cooking utensils,
dishes, clothes for the winter.
A stove. All they treasure.

The wife, following,
the bulge of the next child
large. Fearing the need
to stop, to bury it in the lonely sand.
Her bonnet faded pale
by relentless sun.
Her mother's tea pot wrapped
in wool blankets, fragile
as hope.

*Road Trips: Poets Respond to Travel on Life's
Highways & Byways* (Highland Park Poetry)   2024

ABOUT THE AUTHOR

Peggy Trojan published her first poem in 2010 when she was seventy-seven and has since been published in a wide variety of journals and anthologies.

Peggy's first chapbook *Everyday Love*, a collection of poems about her parents, placed second in the Wisconsin Fellowship of Poets chapbook contest in 2015 and was a finalist for the Northeast Minnesota Book Awards. Her chapbook *Homefront: Childhood Memories of WWII* was published by Evening Street Press. Peggy's full-length collection *Essence* won publication by Portage Press. Her third chapbook *Free Range Kids*, published by Evening Street Press, won the Helen Kay Chapbook Contest. In 2018, Peggy compiled her poems into a 236-page book called *All that Matters* so her family and friends would have most of her work in one place.

Peggy's fourth chapbook *River* recounts her life of growing old with her husband David, and how their existence was suddenly interrupted by his diagnosis of Lewy body dementia*. David passed away in September 2020. *River* was recognized by the Wisconsin Library Association as an Outstanding Book of Poetry for 2021 and won second place in the Wisconsin Fellowship of Poets' chapbook contest.

In *PA*, Peggy pays tribute to her father Wayne Lundeen who lived a full life and strongly influenced her with his values and actions. PA was the Honorable Mention poetry book in the 2022 Northeast Minnesota Book Awards and won second place in the Wisconsin Fellowship of Poets' chapbook contest.

Peggy's sixth chapbook, *The Dance*, was published in 2023 and is a compilation of poems that looks back at a long life and ponders the present.

Reflections contains the majority of Peggy's poems from recent years published in print or online in an effort to collect her work in one place.

Peggy resides in the house she built with David, her father, and family on a tributary of the Brule River in Brule, Wisconsin.

Made in the USA
Columbia, SC
28 September 2024

42375984R10026